Instructions Respecting
The Art Of Transmuting
And Ameliorating
The Metals

William Baron Von Shroeder

© 2023 Culturea Editions
Texte et illustration de couverture : © domaine public
Edition : Culturea (Hérault, 34)
Contact : infos@culturea.fr
Retrouvez notre catalogue sur http://culturea.fr
Imprimé en Allemagne par Books on Demand
Design typographique : Derek Murphy
Layout : Reedsy (https://reedsy.com/)
Dépôt légal : janvier 2023
Tous droits réservés pour tous pays
ISBN : 9791041942657

Instructions Respecting The Art Of Transmutation And A meliorating The Metals

The following translation is interspersed with quotations from Basil Valentine, T. G. Tugel, M. Pott etc. Accompanied with remarks by the translator. The remarks are included in parinthesis (thus) to distinguish them.

My intention is not to enter into Disputes as my time is too precious for that; what I propose writing I have seen and partly elaborated myself, and am still employed in bringing the same to perfection.

Although it is hardly worth a Man's while to bring any proofs concerning the Reality and Existence of our Art, yet if we were not to mention something, our silence would by many be deemed inability, therefore almost against our inclination we see ourselves obliged to relate a few Tracts, the Truth of which cannot be taken in question.

It is positively known that Theophrastus Paracelsus was well acquainted with the knowledge of transmuting mercury and lead into gold; this has even been attested by some of his enemies.

Raymundus Lullius transmuted a great quantity of lead into gold, which he gave to King Henry of England, to enable him to assist other powers in retaking the Holy Land from the Turks; this is well authenticated in History, and yet there exists yet a letter written by the same Raymundus Lullius to King Henry, where he comments having furnished gold to the King, as he employed it to the contrary to agreement, to go to war with France. Through this Letter Raymundus Lullius was put in the Tower of London, as a prisoner of State.

I have seen several Rose Nobles, which have all been made of that gold procured by Lullius. But what need have we to quote Examples of remote times? We have plenty of a later date, and even have no occasion to go out of Germany!

Whosoever doubts, let him go to Dresden in Saxony, and examine the so-called Gold-House, and let him enquire what has been translated in that Laboratory, in the times of Elector Augustus, Electoress Anne and their Son Christianus I, and let him ask from where proceeded those superb buildings seen at Dresden? If he, the unbeliever, wants still stronger proofs, let him go to the Electoral Libraries and enquire for the Chemical Acts and Journals of the Middle and latter End of the 15th Century, and if he goes to the Secret Chancery, he will see such an immense quantity of manuscripts and large volumes, some written by the Elector Augustus himself, wherein he may read how from time to time the tinging powders were elaborated and what immense quantities of gold was procured thereby weekly, that he may well be astonished, as we have been ourselves.

On the other hand in the Chamber of Public Accounts, where all the immense Expenses were set down, for erecting such magnificent buildings, he will not find a single Groschen set down as received for defraying such enormous Expenses.

Such Buildings were the Palaces, Stables, Gardens, Augustburgh, etc.; for erecting them, the Expenses flowed from the Secret Chancery, as they received it from the Gold-House.

It is well known at Vienna that Baron Chaos had a Powder in his possession, wherewith he made projection in presence of our late Emperor Ferdinand III, when His Imperial Majesty who was a Lover, a wise and good man; made Baron Chaos a Count of the Empire.

Baron Chaos had not made the Tincture himself, but had received it from an Earl of Mansfield, who was a General at Raab in Hungary, who died, and the Tincture fell into the hands of Chaos.

There is at this day a gold medal in the Imperial Cabinet of Curiosities which attests, that that gold was made out of mercury in the presence of his Imperial Majesty Ferdinand III.

The many projections which have been made at Vienna with a Tincture of the well known Wentzel by his present Imperial majesty and by many others, and that the said Wenzel was made Baron of Reinburg, are so fresh in memory, that it is superfluous to repeat it here; although Baron Reinburg could not prepare the tincture no more than Baron Chaos, which is well known.

What Dr Helvetius at the Hague related to me with his own mouth, many years ago, when I paid him a visit, every one may read in his own publication, The Golden Calf.

Baron Wagner Ecko, who departed this life only last year, had a Tincture, whereof 1 grain transmuted 3-1/2 lott of any imperfect metal into pure gold. Consequently 1 part transmuted and fixed 1680 parts.

The whole City of Prague, many wise men, and men of rank can testify the truth of this, to whom the Baron showed the Transmutation without fear, and made them presents of small pieces, as testimonies of the Truth of the Art.

So much I know that the Baron's Tincture was elaborated Via Universali; a Mercurial Water was made first and then united with a Sulfur or most subtle Crocus of Gold, ad observing the degrees of fire, it passed through the black, white, yellow and red colors and was multiplied by the same Mercurial Water. This Tincture was of a very fiery color.

The Baron de Wagner Ecko's Furnace was an Athanor built of bricks and was fired with charcoal.

There are at present living possessors, some of them are my friends, others I only know, but I cannot divulge their names, whilst they are living.

I know one amongst them, but a very few years ago, was very poor, but at present is a very different man.

Frankfurt and Augsburg can tell long stories concerning this man's gold and silver. At first I would not believe him, that he was a possessor, because he did not immediately discover himself, and I knew his former Indigence!

Men generally make use of their good fortune according to their genius and natural capacity.

It is yet fresh in memory, that not long ago a Hollander, a goldsmith, of the name of Sommer resided in Vienna, who fixed out of a Tincture of Mercury 4 into pure silver.

I have made the Experiment with my own hands; I have seen his Medicine under two forms.

The first, whereof he gave some to the Lord Bishop at Neustadt, was a grey powder, which I have dissolved in common water, and found that it consisted of 3 parts o salts and 1 part of a fixed white metallic essence.

The other Medicine was a red fixed glass, whereof he gave some to one of the Commissaries of his Imperial majesty.

I have once seen the operation of the Medicine, which was performed in 16 hours, in a strong fire, in the open air, on account of the poisonous fumes.

The Basis of the Medicine was a fixed arsenic, which fixation, I found, had been made with borax in a crucible.

The tinging powder proceeded from a sublimate of copper or Verdigris and from lead; antimony.

In out days we also had in Moravia a certain person, who during a cementation of 7 hours, after having Cemented some silver previously in order to render it compact as they call it, enriched it so much with a graduating powder, that 3 parts out of 4 were fixed and tinged into good Gold, of nearly 24 carat.

To do still more than relate Facts, we will communicate here an experiment, which will prove at once that our Art is true.

Experiment to Demonstrate the Possibility and Truth of Metallic Transmutation

Take fine silver 1 part, Hungarian copper 2 parts, or according to this proportion q:p.

Melt the 2 metals together, then granulate the mass, as is customary, as much as this weighs take amalgamated mercury sublimate, mix it well in a retort, so that it may lay in the retort, as if it were SSS.

Place the retort in a sand heat, and distill the mercury from the mixture into a Receiver with water, and you will find and see the matter in the retort flowing together like a gum, which is of as easy fusion as Bees wax and burns if set on fire.

This matter project into melted lead on a test and cupel it, and you will obtain a pure metal, which dissolve in Aqua Fortis, and a small proportion of fine gold will fall down in the AF solution; half of your silver is become volatile, and by this volatilization of silver you might learn something. I could communicate something useful here, if I had a mind to communicate indiscriminately, but I only want to prove here the possibility of a partial transmutation of some small quantity of silver into gold by the power of power of the sublimate of mercury.

I request also the unbelieving Chemical artists or such Lovers as are full of doubts, to try that common and well known

ExperimentwithCinnabar

Take pure fine silver in filing 1 part or 1 j, common cinnabar in longish pieces, as thick as a straw, or a little thicker, aa.

Dry the cinnabar in the white of an egg, then roll them about in the filings of silver, so that plenty of the silver filings sticks on the cinnabar all around. Place these pieces into a glass body, and make an even SSS with filings and pieces of cinnabar, and lay them very regularly.

Apply an alembic on the body, unluted; put the body deep into the sand, and in such a manner that you may have it in your power to give fire at the top over the alembic, as well as under the body. Thus arranged begin with you fire at the top, but very gradually the first 2 hours, afterwards give fire below, which increase until the mercury in the cinnabar comes over into a Receiver half full of water; mind that the pipe of the alembic goes deep into the receiver and that you lute nothing, or your vessel must absolutely fly to pieces.

In a day the operation is performed.

After the vessels are cooled, take your silver out of the body, which is reduced to ashes. The cinnabar pieces, as only the superfluous mercury is come over, lay entire in the body, and look black like lead.

If you melt this in a crucible, you will find a strange sort of silver, which AF dies not dissolve as it is Luna Fix.

Now tell me how this Pythagorean Transmutation of Bodies and Spirits has happened?

Ocular Demonstration will now convince you, I hope!

(See Tugel's Experiments with cinnabar and silver and gold. I shall give them hereafter.)

The operation of the Adepts differs according to the subject, which is not always one and the same. (Stahl confirms this)

In respect to Books my opinion is this: Whosoever has a good Foundation, may become more perfect by study, but He that knows nothing, will never become possessed of a Tincture, by reading alone! Because the Philosophers' style is this: They keep the subject a profound Secret, and tell their process enigmatically, and to hinder an experienced operator of discovering their matter, they intermix common operations with AF, mercury sublimate, or SV and thus lead you from one Labyrinth into another, and still they write the Truth, but intermix it with Sophistry.

Where they speak too openly, there is Deception, but where they write enigmatically, there lays concealed the Truth.

The most honest and plainest writers are Raymundus Lullius and Basilius Valentinus, but you read all the good authors and mind there they agree in the main point, and then you must endeavor to obtain a [??] and sublimate of Mercury out of one subject only.

(Mr Tugel gives us such a process, to prepare a genuine sublimate of Mercury and a philosophical salt by one operation only, from crude Red Calaminarus from Aix La Chapelle; this sublimate of mercury, says Mr Tugel, will perform every operation, which even Basilius' sublimate of mercury can possibly do; I shall hereafter give you this process of Mr Tugel with several other valuable operations, from his universal and experimental Chymistry.

Basilius in all his writings has in one particular place only, named the true and most universal subject, cinnabar ore and antimony)

Whosoever takes this mineral subject, will nevertheless be deceived, as Basilius does not tell you the Character nor the Right Time, whereby you are to know and at what time you are to get the Genuine Subject.

Without such knowledge, to know the name of the subject merely, is of no use, as the matter varies in different mines.

If you can get the right subject and know how to extract the sublimate of mercury f=out of it, you have all that is needful.

Bernhardus Trevisanus teaches what to do with your sublimate of mercury more plainly, if you can but obtain his and our genuine universal mineral subject.

Otherwise every subject requires a different operation and purification, which may appear to an unexperienced artist.

(Basilius' Process and Universal Mineral Subject, which is also that of Count Bernard Trevisan, quoted by Baron Schroeder, and is His Favorite Subject also, may as well come in here, as in any other place;)

Basilius' '*Of Natural and Supernatural Things*', Hamburg German edition, 1694, p. 241. This tract is included in '*The Last Will and Testament*' of Basilius Valentinus.

'Take in the name of God a red quicksilver ore, which looks like Cinnabar, and the best gold ore (this is Hungarian antimony), aa, grind them together, before they have been in the fire.

'Pour upon this mixed powders, a powder of mercury made per se out of common purified and sublimed mercury (i.c. mercury sublim.), digest it for a whole month, and you will obtain an extraction, which is heavenly.

'Distill the Liquor gently in Baln. Vaporis, and the phlegma will come over, whilst the ponderous glass remains in the bottom of the glass body.

'This glass dissolves all the metals in a moment.

'Pour gradually and with great caution, 3 times as much rectified S.V. to this glass, digest them together, until the mixture is become blood red, and become perfectly sweet.

'The S.V pour from the glass, and pour fresh SVR upon the same glass, digest again, and the glass will become still sweeter, pour the SV off again and new SV upon the corrosive, and digest, and continue in this manner by dulcifying the glass, until the glass is quite saturated and is become sweet and is red as a Ruby, and transparent.

'After every digestion you must distill the SV from the glass in a Baln. Vap.; which will come over very clear like water.

'Now take the remaining ruby red transparent Liquor and pour it into a retort upon calcined **, and distill in ashes pretty strongly, and the sublimate of mercury will come over into the receiver, and will carry over its own sulfur and salt into one Liquor, while the remaining SV will stay behind with the **.

'If you dissolve gold in this treble or animated sublimated sublimate of mercury, you may fix the whole into such a Tincture, which will heal Diseases and procure Riches abundantly.'

(This is a Via Humida, as are all the processes of Frater Basilius)

Baron Schroeder continues thus: The Rays of the Sun and Moon and the Influences of the Stars act and penetrate the Earth continually by means of Air and Water, and meet towards the central Fire of the Earth. From whence they are repelled in Vapors towards the Superficies or Circumference all round.

In passing they impregnate and inspissate the Subterraneous Water and form it into a Saline Essence. (Remember Becher's Oedipus Chymicus his remarkable expression [Pinguis Terrae, Fat of the Earth] there, in the foregoing ms.)

This Saline Essence is further contracted by succeeding vapors and becomes a ponderous metallic water, which we call Quicksilver, and ought to be named the first metal.

This Mercury, by further inspissation by succeeding vapors is gradually fixed into gold or silver.

The generation of Metals commences towards the Center of the Earth and terminates towards the Superficies. The nearer the Metals lay towards the Superficies, the less they do yield, the reason is, that they are remote fro the Central heat and more exposed to the pressing atmosphere, which hinders their Maturation and Fixation. According to this philosophy the ancients have proceeded, and they have looked for immature Subjects, laying not so deep as the precious Metals.

Take therefore that which in the opinion of men seems vile and unworthy, and let alone that which is precious. (So says De La Brie)

Some men have sought for the first matter and fallen into numberless absurdities.

Some have sought in Urine, in Excrements, in Hair, Dew, in a Slime which is collected in stagnating waters, in various minerals and salts, in Native Cinnabar, in the Regulus of Antimony and other foolish things.

Basilius names the matter openly in one place, where he says: Recipe .p. (p. 241) but as he does not tell the Signs and when you are to take the true matter, you will err nevertheless.

I know some that have this matter, but as they did not take it at the right time, their Labor is in vain.

A great difficulty arises, when you read the philosophers' Books, that they have not every one made their Stone or Tincture from the most Universal Mineral Matter, therefore their operations and processes differ, and their Tinctures also, so that the one does not tinge so highly as the other, nor does every Tincture act on all metals, as the most universal does and ought to do. Therefore one philosopher does not always write like the other concerning his first matter or subject and process, which is to be noted to avoid errors.

In regard to the Most Universal Subject out of which Raymundus Lullius, Bernhardus Trevisanus and Basilius Valentinus have made their most universal Tincture, it is named Electrum Immaturatum.

(Now we are as wise as we were, before we heard this name!)

Art must begin where Nature left here work unfinished, this is the plainest Description the philosophers have ever given us of this universal matter.

There are many wonderful opinions concerning the most universal subject of the Philosophers; I for my part am not inclined to deny or contradict what I have never experienced; It is certain, that there is and does exist, independent of our universal mineral subject, a universal sublimate which infuses and insinuates itself into every matrix, and from which sublimate all Things have their Life and Existence. It is a pure, subtle, vivifying sublimate; I have some knowledge of the virtues and powers of this sublimate, in regard to vegetables, animals, and minerals, and I suppose some know how to do more with this universal sublimate than I do.

Some receive this sublimate in the form of water, some like a Salt, when the Sky is serene and clear, either by means of particular glasses by applying heat, or by laying certain Magnets, such as Mumia, human blood, Minerals or Metallic ashes; or by means of mirrors, attracting that sublimate by night and by day which must be putrefied and purified which purification is a Master piece, as the Signs of perfection and purity are well to be minded; afterwards it is to be multiplied by its own principle in Infinitum and must lastly be fermented with gold and silver therefore I will not disturb any one's good Ideas concerning such a most universal principle or Spirit, if he has more knowledge of it, than I have; and I must confess, that Sublimate Mundi has of late given me many serious Thoughts! But there is another matter in the mineral Kingdom wherein that same universal Sublimate Mundi is most plentifully infused, and wherein he dwells undetermined and is in Spiritual operation and in full course to become a Metal, yet has never been a Metal yet nor even a Mineral.

This is our true and genuine matter; some have named it Lutum Auri.

ProcesstoObtaintheSublimateofMer curyoutofOurMatter

Take the Matter, which Basilius Valentinius (p. 241) has named, and mind that it be an Unripe Electrum, and you cannot err, the operation teaches itself.

Without Mercury nothing can be done in our Art, therefore bend all your thoughts on Mercury.

Est in Mercurius quiequid quarant Sapientes! Nothing in the World has such a power to open Metals radically as Mercury; But we do not mean Vulgar Mercury, but our Sublimate of Mercury, although with Vulgar Mercury our Sublimate of Mercury is multiplied in quantity in Infinitum. Our Sublimate of Mercury converts vulgar mercury into its own nature, and in the same manner does out mercurial Sublimate transmute gold and every metal into its own nature, because it is Primum Ens of Metals.

This is Count Bernard Trevisan's Fountain or Solvens, flowing from a beautiful 7 fold radiated Star prepared from a highly purified heavenly Vitriol.

This matter must be taken in its Elevation that is not before it is ripe.

Seek therefore this matter in an open unlocked subject, early in the morning towards the day, do not understand these words wrongly although the great and Wise do not esteem this thing, and throw it away; you take the shell and let them keep the Kernel.

Try it by fire and water, and the smoke and ill smell will teach you, what you have to hope or expect from your matter.

The Color is beautiful, and shows by the royal garment, that something great is hidden therein. Follow him, until you see the Star of the Wise men, because this is an infallible token of approaching Felicity; but I warn you not to be led astray by the Star of Antimony, as happened to Dr Herdott, because it is not every Star, that shows the right path. But that Star alone, which comes from the East, and did never fall on the earth, but remains standing right over the House, wherein the King of the World was born. Our matter has been generated by the Rays of the Sun and the Moon, and consists of Water, which on account of its internal Form is not yet inspissated.

Our Matter Speaks thus:

Because I was never born, they made me a King. If my mother had brought me into the world, my Crown would have been lost,

It is true, no man values me, because nothing is made out of me, but I am esteemed and valued where the Stone of the Philosophers is prepared.

Second Process Concerning the Preparation of our Sublimate ofMer cury.

Iodocus von Roche has, in his process, plainly described the Extraction of the Mercurial Sublimate. (You have that process in Coelum Philosophorum ms.)

Take our philosophical Nitre, which is as heavy as Lead, but without taste or sharpness, extract out of it a central salt and make thereof a troubled slimy water, rectify it until it is perfectly transparent.

With this sublimate extract its own sulpurous anima, mind yourself, because it is a strong poison. Rectify it of its Faeces and your Sublimate of Mercury is made and Basilius his liquid Key obtained, it is a crystalline transparent Water, ponderous as Lead, and its Color is deeply tinged like gold.

ItsUse .

In this Sublimate of Mercury all metals do melt and dissolve like Ice in Water. Nay vulgar mercury melts therein and is radically dissolved therein, and by such a solution of Mercury Communis our Sublimate of Mercury is multiplied in Infinitum.

The preparation of this Sublimate of Mercury is the great Secret of the Philosophers; on this head they are all silent, and although I write somewhat darkly myself, yet it will be clear enough to those that have learned from my writings to know the True Most Universal matter, as our matter shows itself what must be done therewith.

I call it by its proper name a Sublimate of Mercury, which others have expressed by enigmatical names; Now as in the preparation of this Sublimate of Mercury does consist the first work, therefore be diligent and pay attention to this first operation, which may be done very well in two months time.

The Sublimate of Mercury speaks thus:

I am a wolf who devours all things; I thirst after the blood of my children (the metals) therefore I am called the Devourer of Children. I eat, kill and tear to pieces, and return Life to those I have killed.

Nothing can live without me, and all that dies, I kill.

Whatsoever desires Life, must first be buried within me. All that is living calls me Father and is daily nourished by me; yet no one knows how to obtain me except he has stripped me first of my Coat. Therefore it happens but seldom that any man obtains a sight of me.

(I have never been able to discover the Mineral Universal Subject of Baron v. Schroeder. I have always doubted between Calminasis, Cinnabar Ore, and Auripigmentum or Orpiment. As far as my knowledge reaches they are all three valuable Subjects, but after all, not one of the three might be the right matter used by Baron Schroeder, Count Bernard and many others, amongst the more modern adepts. In order to make this ms more complete, I will give you what I find in Pott's Chemistry concerning orpiment, but first I'll explain Baron Schroeder's own process, as applicable to Orpiment, as far as I am able, although in some places it seems as if he meant cinnabar ore.

You have observed that the Baron says that Basilius names it openly, where he says:

Recipe or take in the name of God a Red Quicksilver Ore which looks like cinnabar, and the best gold ore, which you can find.

What can we make of this else by native cinnabar and Hungarian antimony, which generally contains gold.

Now we must mind that Basilius extracts these two ores with a mercurial Liquor made of mercury sublimate. Observe that cinnabar native or artificial consists of mercury and sulfur. Antimony consists of arsenic, sulfur and mercury. Orpiment consists of arsenic and sulfur.

Note further that sulfur and mercury or sulfur and arsenic are the first seminal principles of all the metals. These two principles are certainly the most homogeneous and most natural Keys to dissolve the metals radically, in order that death and Regeneration may follow.

Baron Schroeder calls his subject an unripe Electrum, so does Paracelsus who names it Electrum Minerale Immaturum. Auripigmentum as well as cinnabar ore and antimony is an Immature Electrum, where the first metallic principles are found, but no metal yet brought to perfection by nature. Such ores as actually contain metal, can not be called Electrum Immaturum!

Then he says 'without Mercury nothing can be done', note this on account of Basilius' process and Pott's, hereafter.

What he means by Sublimate of Mercury, is Spiritual Mercury, or the Mercurial Vapor, either before it is running mercury, or running mercury reduced into a mercurial water or sublimate, as Basilius made one of mercury sublimate, for extracting the mercury and sulfur out of his two Ores.

Concerning the multiplication of his sublimate of mercury by vulgar mercury in Infinitum, Ripley mentions the same of his mercurial water, if you remember. He says that his sublimate of mercury is the Primum Ens of Metals; so is every Mercury of animated by sulfur, so is cinnabar, so is antimony, so is orpiment.

Further he says:

Take for this matter in an open unlocked subject, Early in the Morning towards the Day. (Orpiment is extremely open, and comes from the East, from Turkey)

Take the Shell, and let them keep the Kernel. (This I do not understand.)

The smoke and ill smell will teach you. (This is applicable to orpiment)

The Color is beautiful, and shows by the Royal garment, that something great is hidden therein. (Native orpiment is a most beautiful gold colored ore, foliated or interleaves with Scarlet and gold Colored Leaves.)

Follow him until you see the Star of the Wise men. That Star alone which comes from the East shows the right path. (It seems that he has made a Regulus Orpiment Stellatus which can be done, as Pott says; the Star coming from the east, may allude to the subject coming from the Levant, from Turkey, as we have very little of it in the West of Europe, as Mr Pott observes.)

(Where the matter speaks... I do not understand the meaning.)

TheSe condPr ocess

Take our philosophic Salt, which is as heavy as lead. (Orpiment is nothing near so ponderous as lead, not even as heavy as antimony).

Without taste or sharpness. (So is orpiment.) Extract out of it a Celestial Salt, and make thereof a troubled Slimy or viscous water, rectify it, until it is perfectly transparent. (This is the sublimate of mercury, or Mercurius Philosophorum Simplex.)

With this sublimate extract its own Sulphureous Anima; mind yourself, because it is a strong poison. (Now it is Mercurius Philosoph. Duplex, Sive Animatus.) Rectify it of the Faeces, etc.

It is a Crystalline transparent Water, as ponderous as Lead, and its Color is deeply tinged like gold.

(Now we must examine what Mr Pott teaches us in *Dissertations Chymiques De Moni Mr Pott*, Tome 1, page 140, Paris, 1759. Says Mr Pott: 'Risigallum or Auripigmentum is a mineral of a gold color, divided in Saffron and Scarlet Colored Lamella, proceeding from the sulphurous Vapors combined with the volatile mercurial very penetrating Spirits, which renders this mineral extremely proper to open the metals. Some have called it Sandarach.

(Plinus in his 33 *Book of Natural History*, says that there exists a process whereby gold is made by means of orpiment; a process which invited the Emperor Caligula, a prince very covetous of Riches, to cause some men to work a great quantity of orpiment; by which operation perfect gold was procured, but so small a quantity that the Emperor had reason to repent of his avarice.

(Nevertheless 14 [??] weight of orpiment had been converted into gold. This process has never been attempted since says Plinius.

(There is in Turkey a single vein of orpiment, which furnishes all what is sold in Europe. (There is also a Factitious Orpiment made and sold in London, which the painters use.)

(Orpiment is a brittle ore, and disposed in Lamella like talc, whose leaves are strewn with sandy particles; its color is a fine yellow of a greenish Hue; some parts are frequently of a beautiful Scarlet Color.

(This kind of Sandarach is preferred above others by Alchymists. This Sandarach by its beautiful Color resembles native cinnabar.

(It is a mineral resulting from a superficial mixture of arsenic and sulfur.

(The sulfur is composed of a phlogistic earth and the universal acid. The arsenic is composed of vitrifiable earth and of a great quantity of volatile, fluid mercurial earth. Or in plain terms: its arsenic is composed of a metal and of the sulfureous mercurial earth found in Sea Salt.

(The Mercury of the Philosophers is also composed of this earth united to the purest mercurial principle. (Says Mr Pott.)

(Orpiment contains a metallic mercurial substance; when treated in the water with soap and tartar, it furnishes a regulus as brilliant as fine silver, but so subtle, that the fire consumes it in time. Sand and concentrated fixed alkaline Lyes dissolve it, as well as they do arsenic.

(If you fulminate orpiment with nitre, the sulfur in the orpiment is destroyed, and there remains an arsenical regulus fixed by the alkalized salt.

(This matter mixed with mercury in fusion, renders it white, but takes away its malleability. Orpiment melted with fat, or soap, or oil of tartar or any fixed alkali, observing the danger of its poison, gives a metallic brilliant regulus.

(The sulfur unites with the fixed alkali and forms a scoria, high colored, the same as the Scoria of antimony.

(Egg shells contain particularly the Most Fixed Vitrifiable Principle.

(From the small pebbles, which the Hen swallows, and which alone gives hardness to the shell; deny the fowls sand or gravel, and their eggs have either no shell at all, or a very soft one, like thin white red leather; I have seen the experiment; Glauber consequently is right, when he speaks so highly of his Liquor and Vitrum Silicus, for fixing of volatile Tinctures; Tugel say the same.

(Sperlingius gives a process to make a mercurial regulus with orpiment; he says; take 8 parts of orpiment, 6 of salt and nitre fulminated together, 4 of Limatura iron, 1 of charcoal, melt these ingredients together in a crucible, but beware of the arsenic fumes, and you will have a regulus.

(The regulus of orpiment as well as the regulus of arsenic penetrates copper and makes it white and brittle, on account of its mercurial earth,

(When such a regulus is melted, it imbibes all the Metals, which you put into it, and those metals, when afterwards treated and distilled per retort with sublimated mercury for a metallic butter in the same manner as if you had used regulus antimony mars.

(The regulus of orpiment or of arsenic absorb metals quicker than the regulus of antimony, and renders the metals more volatile. The arsenic in the orpiment when detached from its sulfur is as violent a poison as common arsenic, for men or beasts.

ButyrumOr piment

(I took 1 part of orpiment finely powdered, and 2 parts of sublimated mercury also in fine powder. I put the two powders into a glass retort, and mixed them by shaking the retort, whose neck must be wide; I have placed the retort in the cellar, where I let it remain 24 hours, to attract moisture; afterwards I placed my retort in a sand furnace, and buried it pretty deep in the sand, I adapted a large receiver and luted the joinings carefully, as the fumes, if they should escape, prove mortal, when received in the lungs.

(I have begun with a very gentle fire at first which I increased gradually; the mass in the retort melts and boils and a sublimate comes over like clear water [arsenic trichloride], whose quantity is astonishing, considering that the orpiment and sublimated mercury are both dry powders.

(I found this sublimate equally abundant, when I had not attracted in the cellar.

(Some call this sublimate, which must afterwards be rectified per se, with the same precautions, an oil or Butyrum.

(Its specific gravity is equal to that of mercury, and it smokes constantly.

(After this sublimate an oil comes over, which floated upon the sublimate, and would absolutely not mix with the sublimate, though I shook the glass above 100 times.

(Increasing the fire I obtained a good quantity of cinnabar, which sublimed itself in the neck and upper part of the retort, and there remain a small residue, containing the sandy earth intermixed with the orpiment.

(Agricola gives the following process; Mix equal quantities of mercury sublimate and native orpiment, finely powdered separately, put the mixed powders into a glass retort, which place in a cellar.

(Then place the retort in a sand pot, adapt a roomy receiver which lute carefully to the retort; begin with a very gentle fire, which do not increase before you see it necessary, and a yellow subtile oil or sublimate will come over, which smokes constantly, and consumes metals like a fire.

(This oil ameliorates silver in digestion, but it is too much volatilized therein, so that it must be refixed, and by these means you obtain a white gold or Luna Fixa.

(Agricola says that the foregoing process is of Poppius; he adds that [missing] is blackened by this process but not enriched with gold, and that there is no benefit from this digestion. He adds that this Liquor has some rapport with Butyrum Antimonii, and that if you cohobate this yellow oil or sublimate several times upon its own faeces, your oil will become of a ruby color. If you distill this oil or sublimate from Emeril (iron) this matter will give you an oil as red as blood. Agricola says also: That he knows, that orpiment, antimony and mercury sublimate mixed, distilled and cohobated upon their own faeces, in order to impregnate the sublimate with its own fixed sulfur, contained in the faeces, produces a dark red oil, which always gives proof of gold, in small quantities.

(By means of this red body, the partial transmutation of silver into gold is certainly demonstrable.

(Baron Schroeder, whom we have quoted several times, tells us, that some distill orpiment with mercury sublimate, until they obtain therefrom a gold oil, wherein they digest a Calx of silver; but the Baron adds: that 'the small trifle of gold obtained by this process, does not pay its expenses.'

(This is what I have collected from Pott: It seems the process of making a Butyrum orpiment, which is done in one day, cannot be that of Baron Schroeder, which takes two months, besides that we are by no means certain that orpiment is the Baron's Subject.

(Baron Schroeder continues thus:)

Whosoever wants to make a Tincture, must get a Mercurial Menstruum, which has the power to open and destroy metals, to extract their sulfurs, and to unite and form with tem a Chaos.

This Mercurial menstruum can be made universally out of the Primum Ens of Mercury, that is out of the Limus, as we have mentioned before, and this is the most perfect process, by which afterwards a universally tinging medicine is made. Those who prepare a sublimate of mercury from any other Electrrum Immaturum obtain only particular and not universal tinctures.

There is nothing nearer related to metallic Mercuries than urinous sublimate. The urinous sublimates and salts reduce metals either into an irreducible matter or into a running Mercury, according to the knowledge and application of such urinous salts. Note! That Mercury is the principle out of which the tinging and transmuting power does proceed. In all Alchymical operations you must also observe:

1. Not to undertake destructive calcinations of metals, which in resolving the bodies destroy the metallic Mercury.

2. To purify your materials as much as possible, and to rectify every Thing.

4. Most Labors depend upon the Composition of the 3 principles, therefore nothing must be rejected from the matter, but the Faeces.

I do not doubt but there are other methods to elaborate Tinctures! Who has the means and time, and lives long enough to try every process? As Nature is inexhaustible!

What I have written, I have either seen or elaborated with my own hands.

Anyone that possesses the sublimate of mercury, can very soon accomplish particular Transmutations, independent of the Great Work; particulars flowing from the genuine Fountain are profitable, others are not so.

It is also true, that the power to attract and communicate the Solar Sulfur ca proceed from no other but the Mercurial Principle. This is in every metallic body, and by this particular Tinctures can be made; because the Philosophical Mercury shows itself in various shapes and Forms, and in as many different powers; sometimes as a running Mercury, at other times as a dry arsenical mercury, at other times as a humid sublimate of Mercury; therefore a practical Philosophers sees the Sophic Mercury in a different Form, according to the matter he works upon.

The true Sophic Mercury does Heat Itself and is a Fire. Vulgar mercury is cold.

Without a Mercurial medium it is difficult or perhaps impossible, to elaborate either particular or universal Tinctures.

The Sophic Mercuries must be impregnated with a pure Solar Sulfur, which Sulfur must be taken from such bodies as possess a Solar Sulfur: Be not surprised, if I class the urinous salts among the mercurial menstruums! Isaac Hollandus extracted the metallic Mercuries with urinous menstruums.

1. The Art of all particular medicines consists in that the Sulfurs be extracted out of metallic bodies, radically opened.

2. That such Sulfurs be highly purified and separated from all terrestrial Faeces.

3. That your sublimates, although they should be corrosives, be prepared from purified materials, and separated from all phlegma.

4. That if silver is to be transmuted by a particular Tincture, such silver be first prepared.

Amongst all chemical Labors Cementation is the most difficult; there is no man who can call himself a Master in Cementation.

The safest and surest particular Transmutations are such, where, in Via Humida, two Liquors are digested and matured together.

The Solar Sulfur is found in other metals and minerals as well as in gold.

About 15 years ago I presented the King (about 1669) of England a Goblet of Ruby Glass, which glass I had tinged by projection.

Those that know how to elaborate a mercurial menstruum from man's urine, if they know how to apply it, they may obtain universal Tinctures, and they will see such curious phenomena, as Tinctures entirely metallic do not produce.

Our universal mineral matter, whilst in its crude state, has lately made a great noise in Germany amongst some physicians.

In England that same matter has also lately been praised by physical people above other medicines.

Yet no body knows what he has in hand, they undertake preparations and corrections, and they do more harm than good, in spoiling the matter.

If they took the matter in its crude state, and used it so, provided they knew how to choose and select the genuine matter, they would effect much more good.

In England our matter is dear and scarce, but in Germany abundant enough, and whosoever know it well, finds more of the true mater than of the false or spurious.

Berhard Trevisan and the little treatises Enchiredion Physicae Restitutae and Arcanum Hermeticae under the name of Spes Mea In Ango, have described our process wit our matter as plainly as possible.

Finis.

Anonymous: Dr S. Bacstrom's Commentary on the Work of VonSchr oeder

Dr Bacstrom's remarks on the Baron's process are very ingenious, but, nevertheless, I would explain his meaning differently; it is little wonder that the meaning of the alchemists should be often mistaken, by even the most acute and discerning; for, though in some points they were pretty generally agreed, their philosophy was erroneous in many particulars and hardly any two of them had exactly the same system, and, besides, they wrote designedly in an obscure style. To comprehend their writings it is however necessary to have some knowledge of, and to explain them by their own philosophy, otherwise they will remain forever impenetrable: It is also necessary that their quibbles be guarded against.

In the work before us there is no small share of sophistry. The author says that some searched for the First matter 'in Cinnabar, in the Regulus of Antimony and other foolish things', and, afterwards, 'I warn you not to be led astray by the star of antimony as happened to

Dr Herdott.' And yet it will appear, from what follows, that his first matter is neither more nor less than antimony.

The quibble lays here: Antimony reduced to regulus per se will exhibit a star, but this is not 'the star that comes from the east', 'the star of the wise men', for such a regulus would be unprofitable in this work. The east means the eastern sign Aries: in this house, according to Eirenaeus Philalehtes, the Sulfur necessary to coagulate the mercurial sublimate was found by the wise men; now Aries is the house of Mars: consequently iron is the metal that furnishes the active Sulfur. When iron is joined to antimony and the regulus properly purified. It is then the Regulus Antimony-Martis; 'The sevenfold radiated star', the highly purified heavenly [??]'.

According to this author it is not every antimony that is fit to be used in preparing the stellated martial regulus of antimony: 'Take it early in the morning towards the day --- do not misunderstand the words'. That is not the Sulfur only must be found in Aries but the antimony itself in the Morning of the year, when the Sun is in that sign, for he says, before, that 'we know some who had the matter, but as they did not take it at the right time their labor was in vain'. Almost all who have written upon this subject insist upon the necessity of procuring the matter, or at least on beginning the work; when the sun is in Aries or Taurus, though the author of Coelum Philosophorum says if you only proceed right you will succeed in any season'.

When the Baron bids us 'take the shell and let others take the kernel', he only intimates, that antimony is used in this work not on account of the corporeal gold which is to be found in it. Rich specimens are sometimes worked upon for the sake of the gold that may be obtained from them, but the Alchemists employ this subject because of its Mercury and Sulfur, not its external but its metallic Sulfur; nay, they even (according to this author) make use of the scoria itself, and indeed all of them declare that in the first scoria a gold ex martis may be found.

Where he makes the matter speak the language agrees with the philosophy of the Alchemists. The corporeal gold which it contains is the smallest part of its worth --- it contains gold In Potentia, which, by a skillful artist, may be drawn forth in the form of sophic gold; whereas has its mother the Earth concocted it perfectly it would have been born only vulgar gold, and therefore unfit for the Great Work, having no more than a natural perfection necessary for its own formal existence. It might be used as a ferment to receive, itself, a higher power, but has no power to communicate to other metals till it first receives it.

No man values antimony on account of any mechanic use to which it can be applied; for alone, it is useless; and even when used in combination, is applied to hereby any other use than that of hardening lead [or silver]; but though useless in the arts it is esteemed by the Alchemists.

We now come to another quibble; for though Cinnabar be not the Baron's First Matter, Mercury is his Second Matter. 'Bend all your thoughts on Mercury' --- 'Take our philosophical nitre which is as heavy as lead, but without taste or sharpness, and extract out of it (by means of mercury) a central salt'. By extracting a central salt from the All he intimates that the mercury to be employed in this second work must first be sublimed with common salt, by which means the sublimate of salt is united to the mercury in a concrete form, almost or altogether free from humidity. The regulus being distilled with the mercury sublimate a martial butter of antimony is obtained, 'a troubled slimy water which when rectified is perfectly transparent' [antimony trichloride]. With this sublimate extract its own sulphureous anima'; that is: sublime or distill the rectified butter from the first scoria obtained in making the regulus of antimony and mars.

How often he purifies his regulus, how often he rectifies the butter, how often he cohobates the sublimate upon the faeces of the scoriae he does not inform us, but it is probable these operations were frequently repeated as he allows two months for this labor.

When this labor is finished you have then obtained 'the sublimate of mercury Basilius' liquid key. A crystalline water, ponderous as lead; and now deeply tinged like gold'. By the animation received in the distillations from the scoriae --- perhaps after digesting on the same.

He calls this purified, animated Martial butter of antimony 'A Spirit of Mercury', apparently for no other reason but because in distillation it rises and comes over the receiver as any sublimated from matters yielding a sublimate come over by the same process.

Where he makes the mercurial sublimate speak he is only describing the matter by its saturnine characteristics. Antimony belongs to the family of Saturn. Saturn considered as time produces all things, destroys all things, renovates all things; but sublimate mundi is the efficient cause of all these changes. Time as Time does nothing itself: It is in fact only the periods of the operations of sublimate mundi, without which nothing is produced, nothing lives; it kills all that die, but only for this end, that by means of corruption it may produce regeneration and a new life.

What the ancient philosophers thus declare respecting nature in general out author applies particularly to the sublimate of mercury in the labors upon metals; for from mercury they all come, by this sublimate of mercury they may be devoured, and by the coagulation of the same sublimate may afterwards be revived to a more noble existence.

The coagulation is probably accomplished by simply enclosing some of the sublimate of mercury in a spherical glass and then digesting in a proper heat for a sufficient length of time. After the tincture is finished the first time imbibe it with the same sublimate and again digest and coagulate. Repeat the operation till the Tincture is exalted as high as you will it. After the first coagulation it will prove Sophic gold but not a Tincture; after the second it will be a Tincture, and every succeeding imbibition and fixation or coagulation, will increase it not only in quantity but in power.

Finis.

P.S. --- If you employ common gold in the sublimate of mercury the first coagulation will give only sophic gold --- If you work with animated sophic mercury without common gold the first coagulation yields the medicine of the first order, or a Tincture upon 10 parts.

Finis.